CLOSED POEMS

STEKA VANRA

I dedicate this poems to everybody to whom may concern.

Steka Vanra

CLOSED POEMS

Scream

Nobody hear my quiet silent scream

that can be heard by heart but not by ears

during nightmare of life terrible dream

blows me away in a river of tears.

Nobody see my invisible tears

which extinguish that fire while screaming

of not satisfied passions during years

I live in loneliness, dead and dreaming.

Everyone's scream I can hear with my heart

sharing everyone's passions and suffer

drinking that poison of tears and juices.

Everyone's scream is cause for me to start

eat bitter meal on destiny supper

making my heart with more wounds and bruises.

Pressure

When man is broken under the pressure

after something no longer can stand him

to be visible he wants to be sure

because nobody could understand him.

One stupid harmless mistake is enough

to crucify him on cross of malice

in hypocrisy people always laugh

at his face and that is common practice.

But that people are thirsty for his blood

they need it to drink as good medicine

heal and cure themselves from the same sickness.

Of own dirty conscience in filthy mud

they need to throw him down to don't be clean

and lose purity to become needless.

Pigeon

Hello my feather clothed flying friend

I am always happy when I see you

if my life in cage ever goes to end

I know you'll miss me and I'll miss you too.

I reward your friendship with slice of bread

that is small price to pay for happiness

you give to me just becoming my friend

light up the darkness of my loneliness.

When I see you flying over the wall

people build with stones of hypocrisy

in my mind I fly with you in freedom.

In our lives we are not free at all

we are slaves of our prejudices

ruling our own misery kingdom.

Reason

Nobody had any real reason

to take my freedom stealing it from me

and keep me in hypocrisy prison

destroying life, making me dead to be.

Everybody has some legal reason

to capture me in trap of prejudice

catching me is always hunting season

and arrest me in the jail of malice.

What reason can morality police

find to put on my hands heavy handcuffs

of stupidity caused by human fears.

Those who always want bad things to notice

find reason to justify evil staffs

of people who cause suffering and tears.

Book

The most dangerous people in the world

are those who read always only one book

having stupid excuse that it's God's word

at anything else they don't want to look.

All books in the world are written by man

and in each of them is hidden some truth

to read all of that books nobody can

what of that truths is divine absolute.

As more we read we can more to compare

differences make system of values

on that way we can judge what's bad what's good.

All different wisdoms we must to share

switching our wisdom on high volume

only on that way we could understood.

Justice

When poor man steal a little hi is thief

when rich man still a lot he's businessman

never punishment for the same mischief

is the same everywhere for every man.

Who has a little all that is taken

from him with intention to have nothing

but who has a lot to him is given

because he's the one to have everything.

Criminals are involved in politic

while businessmen are involved in the crime

and politicians are deep in business.

For poor people all that is terrific

and they have need all of that to sublime

and having from them empty promises.

Doctors

In every war doctors heal even a

hated enemy's soldier and we

have to pay for every single event

without money one life is ending.

For our doctor we pay everything

we poses only we want us to heal

to be healthy we will give anything

when we pay him the doctor wants to deal.

He can never even for own doctor

have enough money for healing to pay

then remain only one for him to die.

You spend money for weapons but not for

doctors then people can only to pray

helpless and hopeless to weep and to cry.

Nothing

Who nothing possess can nothing to lose

who has too many can lose too many

one who poverty in honesty chose

will be happy even when he's granny.

Who possess nothing can not lose nothing

nothing is not possible to be lost

only who has something can lose something

Then he fights for more whatever it costs.

Nothing can to lose who nothing possess

happy are those people who nothing have

they have nothing to worry about.

To have something is long painful process

in that need for wealth like crazy behave

have nothing to be sorry about.

Always

It's always very hard to make first step

once you make it just keep walking forward

even when you to drink knowledge thirst wept

When death finishes you'll have a reward.

It's always hard to make first step very

it's comfortable in one place to stay

on the right road we will walk merry

will give us protection from the wrong way.

Make first step it's always very hard to

make decision to start any voyage

undecided we lose many chances.

Always before some trip you must start too

to prepare everything and have courage

on music of fate to know all dances.

Small proprietor

When somewhere some rich small proprietor

rather give some extra food to feed pigs

than to poor people can't be quiet for

that giving because rich people need this.

When they give to poor children then it is

something small proprietor remember

that gift erase mistakes and guiltiness

of goodness he becomes a pretender.

Every small proprietor gives to poor

children something only once when they need

something from those gifted children to do.

Small proprietor gives something for sure

When they expect to satisfy own greed

someone has to give back what they must do.

Volition

It comes to the same thing volition is

a delusion cheating us all the time

everybody who drop volition his

delusion makes him commit heavy crime.

The same thing volition is it comes to

cheating us all the time a delusions

with volition and delusion comes too

to think about and make conclusions.

Volition is it comes to the same thing

all the time a delusion cheating us

and everybody whose volitions drop.

Volition to us is always something

that can never without cheating pass

without delusion volition stop.

Wealthy

If you wish to be wealthy man and rich

you must to have mind of some filthy bitch

if treasures of the world you want to reach

you'll have no pleasure swimming on the beach.

To be wealthy man and rich if you wish

you must to lose feeling of compassion

you will catch from fairy tale golden fish

only if fortune is your obsession.

Man if you wish to be rich and wealthy

just forget that there are other people

who share with you the same needs as you have.

Wealthy people in mind are not healthy

for money they can kill and make cripple

in a rude and aggressive way behave.

Rather

Give rather in some alive mouth in

Death we don't need because of that to us

When you feed you climb on high mountain

Of goodness only good people can pass.

You should not go to our funeral

Rather you should go to some baptism

If in your goodness you are not real

You are not selfish in narcissism.

In hungry mouth you will never must

Anything to put when they are hungry

But rather when they are alive to feed.

Rather than to us if you ever trust

You can trust to our mouth angry

Because of your heartless and selfish greed.

Built

To have his body good built for some war

Then that soldier must be without

Mind and emotions to make that war more

Bloody he should never think about.

Without legs to crawl like snake and

To have four arms instead of two to be

Built for danger and don't be shaken and

Ready for terror and horror to see.

He could with two or his arms to shoot and

With two others his arms to throw grenades

Such built everything is that he must be.

He is built to destroy every cute land

And of that people different grand faiths

Without heart and brain all that must be.

Morality

Moral people always in history

Make war in the name of morality

For nation land and faith that's sad story

They write in the book of eternity.

Immoral people always through the time

Just make love in the name of love itself

For moral people that is heavy crime

Must punish them to justify themselves.

Moral persons destroy lives of people

Fighting for some stupid morality

Killing and dying they believe in that.

Immoral people in love are simple

That is naked true in own nudity

During the act of love, life they create.

Freedom

Nobody can take from me my freedom

Even if they put me in dark prison

To be free we must have real wisdom

For that feeling we don't need a reason.

We believe that we are really free

While we are slaves of some faith blood and land

And all our life we strive free to be

Our slavery we can't understand.

Really free people in history

Were crazy tortured arrested and killed

because they were different is not bad.

Tale about freedom is just story

Written with pens of guns and rifles filled

With ink of blood that story is so sad.

Ship

In vain is to have best ship of good wood

Without wind in its back it can't move

In vain is to be always in good mood

anything you can not ever improve.

If you sail on some old ugly boat

And having good wind to push you forward

On surface of destiny you float

wherever you come you'll have a reward.

Ship of your life on wind only depend

And having good wind to push you forward

Wind makes the ship's speed toward direction.

If captain of destiny understand

Between ship and ocean interaction

From the rocky sea find good protection.

Dream

When I sleep and have some terrible dream

As of my reality reflections

Suddenly I wake up with silent scream

And with that realms have strong connections.

When I dive deep in some beautiful dream

And to wake up again I never wish

Flowing carelessly on that lovely stream

In the net of my dream I captured fish.

While spending our life dreaming awake

And waiting our dreams to become true

We don't know what is real, what's a dream.

And when awaken we make some mistake

Then we realize that dream is so cruel

In the cake of our life that is cream.

Dead

You can not kill dead man more then one time

Having nobody and nothing he's dead

For being alive is his only crime

And living life miserable and sad.

Not satisfying any of his needs

Without respect and love man is dead

And trying of goodness to sow his seeds

In return everything is wrong and bad.

To spend empty life between birth and death

And satisfy needs to eat drink and breed

What's the difference he's alive or dead?

But if he spend life having no regret

And fully satisfy his every need

is ready to lay in the final bed.

Power of love

Nobody can destroy you even worse

Making you feel dead and miserable

Than those around you who love you the most

Because of that love that's affordable.

The worst thing is that you know they love you

And you can't even be angry on them

So they over and over surprise you

Like you with that love they always condemn.

If you can be angry you can feel good

But that supreme love always disarm you

forcing you to forgive them all evils.

But if they could ever you understood

They would never again try to harm you

Acting in love to you like your devils.

Prefer

I prefer to die right and free like man

Than to live wrong in cage like animal

My conscience is most valuable gem

Chance to make it dirty is minimal.

I prefer to love people and forgive

Than to hate them for evil and revenge

Only in love I prefer to believe

For most people that attitude is strange.

I prefer to speak truth whatever cost

Than to tell lies for any benefit

That I can achieve lying and cheating.

I prefer to be for most people lost

That is for my happiness deposit

As long as my chest, my heart is beating.

Winner

Every time when I eat my bitter meal

In eve of life on destiny dinner

When divine cook finish that food to deal

If I eat first I will be a winner.

When takes me away of my hard life stream

In river of events I'm good swimmer

At the end of life that terrible dream

With my clean conscience I'll be a winner.

In my need to love and embrace people

To please and satisfy everybody

That makes me the biggest filthy sinner.

When God ask me why answer is simple

Being already dead and nobody

I will finish that race as a winner.

Need you

When I need understanding you judge me

When I need help you give me punishment

And you do everything disparaging

That is your revengeful stubborn statement.

When I need respect back you despise me

When I need just for my love to be loved

With your hatred you always surprise me

And throw me in your dirty conscience mud.

When I need somebody you run away

Make me feeling dead and invisible

Not existing for you before your eyes.

When I need something you take it away

To earn anything is not possible

My every need for you is a surprise.

Crazy

Giordano Bruno was enough crazy

To claim that Earth is not flat but round

And minds of normal people were lazy

They could not accept that crazy sound.

But of that crazy statement of his mind

Those normal people burned him in fire

And that was just excuse for them to find

Good reason to satisfy desire.

Crazy people have need in those madness

For normal people to build construction

Making new values in science and art.

At the end of life they die in sadness

Normal people have the same reaction

To accept ideas they never start.

Afraid

I'm not afraid what they can do to me

I am afraid what I can do to them

Life in fear with dirty conscience to be

Is not worth living and to be condemned.

I'm not afraid to die with clean conscience

I'm afraid to live causing sufferings

Everything we do we face consequence

That is in a chain of destiny rings.

To live causing suffering of people

And spend life living in fear of revenge

We die every moment being afraid.

All fears return back double and triple

To create wisdom and be a challenge

For joys and sufferings we ever made.

Lost

I am now to old to be hired

Nobody wants me to work in my age

And I am too young to be retired

It's early to turn to another page.

Where to go and what to do to survive

Except my life I have nothing to lose

I don't know what to do to stay alive

anything I am not able to choose.

Being lost man nobody can find me

Even if anybody ever try

I lost everybody I love the most.

Nobody see me who is behind me

And nobody can hear me when I cry

Because for everybody I am lost.

Substitute

Everybody can have me who wants me

Sometimes I feel like I am prostitute

Then he throws me away never warns me

Where's nobody else I'm a substitute.

I always try to belong not to have

For me term of friendship is institute

To be everybody's friend must be brave

when using me just as a substitute.

To live without respect and love back

Giving myself generously to you

I have that stupid stubborn attitude.

But instead to kiss me you bite my neck

And I never know what I have to do

but to be an eternal substitute.

Categories

Oral people want to taste everything

To feel flavor of life always they try

And if sometimes they miss to taste something

They fall down in sadness and start to cry.

Phallic people have need to penetrate

Everywhere and to be always in charge

They have never patience to concentrate

Having need to grow and to become large.

Vaginal people have need to enjoy

To be spoiled and everybody please them

They try to find in everything pleasure.

While anal people everything destroy

They eat others and they try to squeeze them

To fill those asses they have no measure.

Water

Throw diamond in water it will sink

But throw shit in water it will float

Not welcome are people who know to think

But welcome are those stupid like goat.

In water of life if you want to swim

You must eat every small fish like some shark

Where you will finish in destiny stream

Depends only on how you embark.

In water of life you are good swimmer

If you swim over small and dying fish

Swimming carelessly over those bodies.

In destiny water you are winner

And you will fulfill every dirty wish

Having for other people no worries.

Call

When I call God he never comes to me

When I call devil he is always here

Every time when I need with God to be

Instead of him devils always appear.

We spend our life giving hope in God

At the same time devil in us give hope

Believing blindly in him and his word

Blind we put on our neck devil's rope.

God is def and blind for our suffer

He gives us hope for salvation in death

Then we will maybe go to paradise.

Devil offers to us tasty supper

Eating and drinking we lose our breath

Where is heaven, where's hell? That's a surprise.

River

We who always straighten curvy river

Expose ourselves to real danger

We who are not taker only giver

live in suffering being a stranger.

But river of life continue to flow

With us or without us in its stream

Being strangers we are condemned to drown

Believing blindly in that river dream.

River in its curvy flow entire

Hide many secretly targeted traps

In all of them it's dangerous to fall.

Flowing toward prejudice empire

Listening always of promises craps

We will never go anywhere at all.

Needs

Wise man has always the same need to hear

While foolish man has always needs to say

While wise man is silent even in fear

Foolish man quiet who can never stay.

Wise man has always the same need to love

While foolish man has always needs to hate

Silence in wisdom for wise is the law

Speaking all the time, foolishness is fate.

Wise man needs everything to understand

For everybody he has compassion

In his pure need to embrace all people.

Foolish has never need to comprehend

Just basic need to satisfy passion

Usually is a moral cripple.

All of us in our lives have same need

But all of us that same need satisfy

In many colorful different ways.

As long we have need to eat drink and breed

Shall we drop deep down or shall we high fly

We create our darkness and bright days.

Wishes

All not fulfilled wishes cause suffering

But fulfilled wishes cause disappointment

When bell of our alarm start to ring

For our wishes we need agreement.

As long we have wishes we all exist

Our wishes make us to be alive

While to fulfillment we always persist

For our happiness with wishes strive.

In absence of all possible wishes

Lays the secret of endless happiness

When we have no wishes we have no pain.

After eating all those tasty dishes

Remain nothing but only emptiness

Causing the fall of tears hot heavy rain.

Enemy

I am to myself biggest enemy

And I must be protected from myself

To destroy myself is my destiny

For guidance of anybody I'm def.

Nobody in this world can more harm me

Than I who harm myself during my life

Against myself somebody must arm me

With divine wisdom, a sharp cleaver knife.

And so while to myself I make evil

My life pass in waiting for happiness

which by accident always misses me.

I am somehow to myself own devil

Causing for myself empty loneliness

And making nobody want to kiss me.

People

Small people have needs everything to have

Because of those greedy need to collect

In taking goods like crazy they behave

With reality they can not connect.

Average people have need for hard work

And working hard they seek for salvation

To relax and enjoy for them is joke

of the entire world makes creation.

Big people have needs everything to know

In understanding is hidden all truth

They spend all life exploring and searching.

Knowledge they need everybody to show

And that goal is divine absolute

They can not be ever disparaging.

Tears

Ever since man start to believe

In woman's tears by his own stupid choice

All the time must everything to forgive

Having no permission to raise his voice.

Man's tear is heavy like a solid stone

When he squeeze it painfully from his eye

After that he falls down from his mail throne

And to his man's pride he must say goodbye.

Only child's tear is completely sincere

Only to that is possible to trust

When it starts to flow from the wounded hearts.

Immediately when child's tear appear

To wipe it out from face we all must

When some source of pain to produce them starts.

Man who start to believe in woman's tears

Become forever slave of those well springs

And when woman's weeps enter in man's ears

Eternal suffering for him brings.

Every time when some strong man start to cry

That means for him something is very hard

That keep him down he never again fly

And he can not leave own misery yard.

Innocent children's tears fall on the souls

Of evil people who always cause them

Giving terrible pain to those angels.

Who kick children like they are playing ball

Neglecting fact that they are priceless gem

Put those pure hearts in terrible danger.

Imprisonment

All of us are convicted in prison

Because of crime of our existence

For that they always find some good reason

We have no power to give resistance.

We are convicted on the life in cell

And from that cell we can never escape

That's the reason why we can not feel well

Being bound with hypocrisy tape.

Invisible iron bars divide us

With solid locked doors of stupidity

Made with prejudices and from malice.

When in that deep and dark cell invite us

Guardians of foolish morality

To sentence us for life is that practice.

Deserve

I can not be enough evil and bad

To deserve from anybody respect

That makes me to be in bad mood and sad

Pleasure in anything I can't detect.

I can not be enough bad and evil

To deserve back from anybody love

When I face sometimes demon or devil

can't be touched with a dirty handed glove.

As much somebody I try to respect

As much somebody I honestly love

Only despise and hatred I receive.

I don't deserve somebody to protect

Me from myself when my destiny flow

Toward happiness I never achieve.

Path

When I walk on path many people passed

That path is under many feet mudded

I always go back in my remote past

When I was loved, rewarded and cuddled.

When I make for myself some brand new path

Many obstacles lay on my new way

Working hard on it and losing my breath

On my path I wish forever to stay.

On busy trafficked path many people

There pass push each other and move away

And always disturbing one another.

If I fall down I will be poor cripple

If I don't know that dirty game to play

Without some friend, lover or brother.

Adore

Those persons who only God can adore

And in the name of Him make all evils

For people they have no love any more

Believing in God they become devils.

But all those people who worship devil

And who spend life without smile on face

Finally to fall in abyss they will

And after them there will remain no trace.

Only those nice persons who love people

Who worship and pray to Goddess of love

Can hope to achieve real happiness.

In that divine love those minds are simple

And when they lay head on deadly pillow

Only after them remain emptiness.

Awakening

Last night I lay down and alive I slept

But early this morning dead I awake

In nightmare of life I screamed cried and wept

to remain awake that I can not make.

All my good and bad dreams look more real

Then my one true life in reality

When provider of dreams finish to deal

Then I'll not believe in morality.

And with my every next awakening

I drive more deep in that dreams of my life

Awaken all my dreams become real.

I continue to dream life suffering

Of wounds made by my bad destiny knife

That cuts me for my awakening meal

Marriage

We all have need with somebody to live

And being together we become one

Sometimes we are given sometimes we give

Our partner can not be anyone.

But when we are alone like we are dead

We have nobody for whom to exist

When we have no one to share our bed

To make our family we persist.

Our marriage building we build with love

With mutual respect and confident

Cemented and sealed with our children.

When somewhere out from marriage we move

To make for our partner measurement

We lose our family for freedom.

Door

When with your leg door of your life you close

With hand you will never again open

When of happiness you have overdose

write the story of your life with a pen.

But when door of your life is wide open

Offers to everybody warm welcome

Everybody wants to return again

To visit you with happiness they come.

Behind heavy door with key and with lock

No happiness singing song and laughter

Neither is life in that cold house not.

Behind door of your life is secret stock

Of causes before to effects after

Making it to be cold or to be hot.

Nobody and nothing

I have nothing I am proud on that

That nothing working honestly I earned

Divine Goddess of wealth I never met

as nobody , a hard lesson I learned.

Without anything I don't worry

Being nobody I am not afraid

And I have no reason to be sorry

Nobody's suffering I never made.

I have nothing to keep nor to tremble

For my own life I don't have any more

Already dead man again can not die.

Being nobody I have no trouble

People not money I always adore

But those bad people always make me cry.

Devil

Good man has power over his devil

Who lays secretly hidden in himself

His food steps are of goodness not evil

And people make him happy with themselves.

Bad man is under power of devil

Who rules with all his dirty acts

And to cause suffering he always will

Misery, those undeniable facts.

All of us inside have god and devil

And all strong power to rule over them

Or they will take power all over us.

If with evil acts our life we fill

With devil himself we will be condemned

When we neglect everything that warns us.

Stomach

When my poisoned stomach start to be spoiled

Over eating all shits (trash) of destiny

And when hot blood in me start to be boiled

Instead of being fat I am skinny.

I forgive evils to everybody

And running back to my past I make move

Can give me medicine anybody

To heal my stomach I can not improve.

If I ever kick out from myself

Of destiny shits (trash) I ever swallowed

I will walk fast like some handsome young man.

I wish to find good doctor in yourself

To heal my stomach you are allowed

Your love as medicine will be omen.

Borrow

I'm seeking desperately to borrow

Not more than just two hundred grams of brain

Without that probably tomorrow

Before the station I will leave the train.

Desperately to borrow I'm seeking

Only half kilogram of happiness

In vain I spend most of my life speaking

to fertile the desert of loneliness.

To borrow I'm seeking desperately

Brain and happiness to maintain my life

And maybe never I will give it back.

That is essence of life ultimately

The same like for husband his beloved wife

To show me the way my head moved by neck

Stop

I had to stop seeing her because I

Couldn't stop seeing her that's the reason

But if I don't stop seeing her then I'll

Commit heavy crime and go to prison.

I stop seeing her because I had to

Do it long time ago in the right time

I can live without air and bread too

without her I would commit a crime.

And because I had to stop seeing her

But I didn't I continue to see

She and I will see her in the future.

I can't stop being the biggest sinner

I am drowning in the tide of love sea

To stop seeing her is not my nature.

Dragons

Children are like dragons they always run

In some danger and during that they laugh

They are always shining like with rays sun

Except when they are sick in bed coughing.

Like dragons they always run children are

Endless source of many funny mischief

When they wake up in the morning then star

Start to shine brighter at what they achieve.

Dragons they always run children are like

Dragon always eager for everything

Everywhere there is everything to see.

When dragon knight in shiny armor strike

Armed with weapon of hate can't anything

Of all children virtues himself to be.

To receive

Who wants just a little will not receive

Anything but who wants a lot will have

Something and what you give when you retrieve

more gifts if you like that behavior.

At least a little will receive who ask

A lot and as more he ask he will more

Receive but if it is his only task

will start to behave like a filthy whore.

Who seek and wants a little he will not

Receive anything because of that must

To ask as much he can and frequently.

To receive something when wrap you that knot

If in giving you never start to trust

That rope of your greed will hang you gently.

Every

Always every hand is beautiful which

Give but hand which receive is beautiful

Only when receive from somebody rich

In my heart, that present is wonderful.

Hand is beautiful which always every

Only cuddle others but never kick

That hand makes everybody be merry

Can heal somebody from hate fever sick.

Which is beautiful always every hand

When it embrace neck of beloved in love

And that kind of hand is made of pure gold.

Every man in love in his marriage land

Can be her pigeon if she is his dove

In the market of love it's for sure sold.

Sailing

Every single sailing has only two

Possibilities to arrive in port

Or to sink on bottom but only who

When onboard they can practice that sport.

And shipwreck is sailing on the bottom

When ship of our life in port of death

Sink down so softly like on cotton

maybe a port of salvation is that.

When you sail on the bottom such sailing

Will stop you in any port to arrive

Maybe that is a port of salvation.

Sailing in the ship of life and failing

To rich the port of happiness you strive

Sink to the bottom is the solution.

Hate

In hate everybody knows people all

Always more easy agree much more than

in love 'cause when hate gives to people call

After that love nobody will thank them.

All loves create suffering to themselves

Hate create suffering to the others

If you recognize hater in yourself

You will never have sisters and brothers.

All people In love always they create

Suffering because of loving creature

They in love suffer only for others.

Every time when with hate people relate

They have before those eyes twisted picture

They forget that they also have mothers.

Every run

Every race of life I always run first

And I always give up before finish

To drink wine of winning I have such thirst

But somehow before me it vanished.

I always run first race of life every

And I give up before finish always

To win at least one race I need very

But I broke my leg when I ran all day.

Every race of life I run first always

And before finish I always give up

I have a thirst to drink after winning.

Every run of life I can have all days

Of the winner I will never lift cup

I must start running from the beginning.

Contents

www.ingramcontent.com/pod-product-compliance
Lightning Source LLC
Chambersburg PA
CBHW031514150726
47990CB00007B/3011